Dedicated to my students
-Mrs. Dorcely

This book belongs to:

_____

This month, the children are learning all about apples with Ms. Annie!

Ms. Annie shows the children pictures of apple trees in different seasons.

Ms. Annie shows the children pictures of apple trees in winter.

Ms. Annie shows the children pictures of apple trees in spring.

Ms. Annie shows the children pictures of apple trees in summer.

Ms. Annie shows the children pictures of apple trees in fall.

Ms. Annie says, "Tomorrow, everyone will bring an apple to class!"

Altogether, the children bring 25 apples.

The children count five yellow apples.

The children count ten green apples.

The children count ten red apples.

The children wash the apples.

The children look at the parts of an apple.

The children see an apple has leaf.

The children see an apple has a stem.

The children see an apple has skin.

The children see an apple has flesh.

The children see an apple has seeds.

The children see an apple has core.

The children taste the apples.

The children make applesauce.

The children make apple pie.

The children make apple juice.

The children make candy covered apples.

The children make apple turnovers.

At the end, Ms. Annie says, "Apples are good for you!"

What else can you make with apples?

What color is your favorite apple?

Draw a picture of your favorite color apple.

What is your favorite food or drink made with apples?

Draw a picture of your favorite food or drink made with apples.

Your turn, name the parts of an apple.

 red apple

 yellow apple

 green apple

 **apples**

 **leaf**

 **stem**

 **seeds**

 **core**

 **flesh**

 skin

 apple turnover

 candy covered apples